STRESSED OUT &
SCATTERBRAINED

WRITTEN & ILLUSTRATED
BY BONNIE BLUE EDWARDS

WALNUT STREET
— **PUBLISHING** —

ACKNOWLEDGEMENTS

Deep thank-yous to those who inspired the tales as well as helped shape this first collection. There were many, strangers and all, but special thanks to:

Elyssa Budd
Travis DeMello
Megan Logan
Katie Manion
Taylor Weaver

Also to Avram Ludwig, who took me on many near-disastrous sailing exploits.
You are forever missed.

INTRO

During the recession of 2010, I moved from Alabama to NYC in pursuit of any kind of opportunity. Fresh in my 20s, I soon began an unpaid internship while working minimum wage at a grocery store. Within the hustle, I scribbled down poems (or rhyming stories, as I prefer to call them) depicting the woes of surviving the Big Apple. Mishaps and adventures such as trying to make friends, navigating subway delays, dating in the urban jungle, and much more. These tales were written instinctually on crumpled sheets of paper or obscure notebooks over ten years. Eventually, in my 30s, I dug up these stories and then, even years after that, I decided, hey, why not try to illustrate them myself? So here you go.

Thank you for taking the time to read. Seriously. Please stay in touch through my Instagram account @bonnieblue952 or at my website www.bonnieblueedwards.com.

To add to your reading vibe or enjoy on its own, feel free to check out this Spotify playlist with some of my favorite tunes circa 2010-2019, at the QR code below.

WHY DON'T YOU JOIN ME FOR A PEE?

Excuse me, pardon me
Close the damn door
I've never even met you before

Yet here I am
Sitting down to pee
I thought I'd turned the lock, you see

You just stand there and stare, all the other café
goers aware
How about you pull up a chair?
If you dare

This isn't my first unlucky lock
In this city, they happen a lot
Or is that just my luck?

WHEN AM I EVER GOING TO HAVE TIME TO DO LAUNDRY?

The clothes on my floor
On my chair and blocking the door
All need to be cleaned
They're making sounds and starting to be mean

They stare and they glare
Their judgement I feel
But come on, you guys, let's be real

The days are too short
The lists of to-dos too long
If I die of dirty clothes, it just might be where I
belong

This is ridiculous
Can't you just please wash yourselves?
Oh how I wish I had magic spells

For laundry, for dishes, for all the tasks
But, alas, I guess it's just too much to ask

Yet the question on everyone's mind is
When am I ever going to have time
To do my laundry?

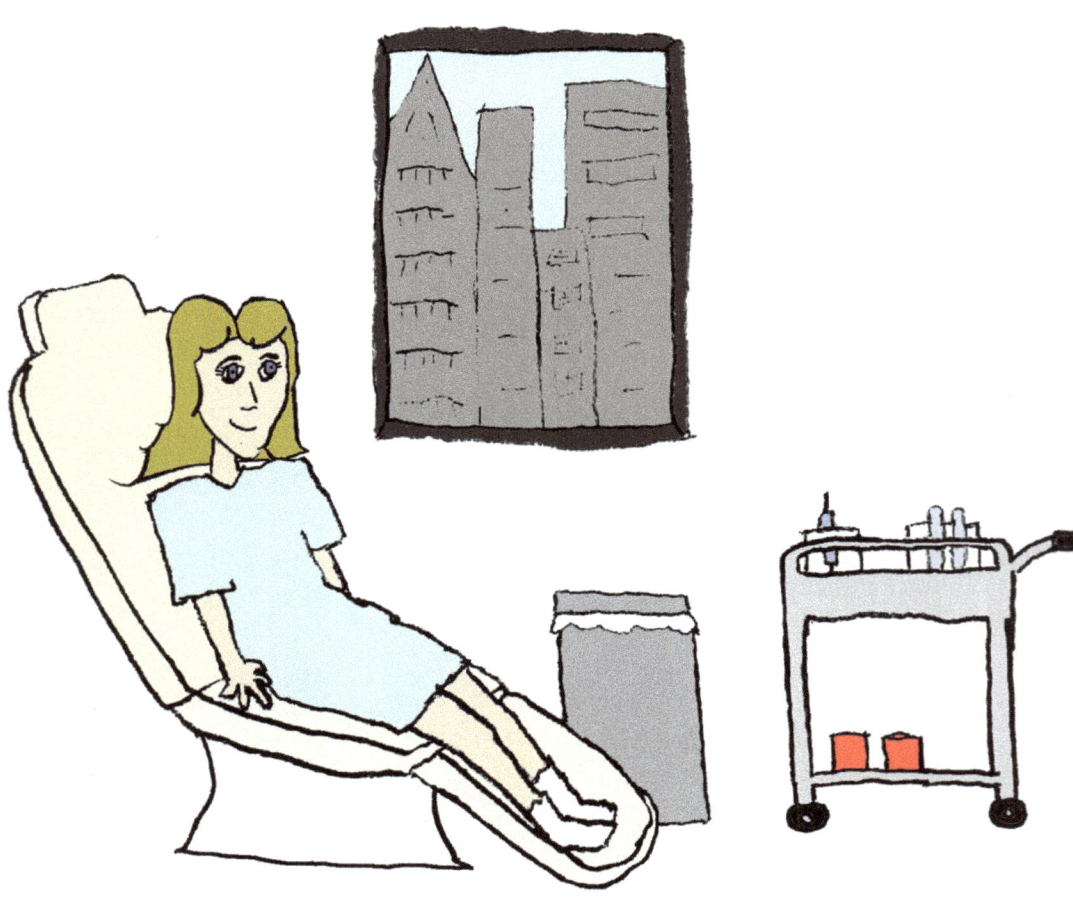

TAKE MY EGGS AND GO START ANEW

Let me tell you something
About a girl and her eggs
They found a home in someone
We just don't know who yet

Her ovaries were nice and largesse
Many follicles did they possess
On top of that, she did not see
Children in her future, so why not let it be

A gift to another, her eggs to you
And the money that she got, will be of use
She'll change her career, she'll fight to be
Someone of use, someone to you and me

So months of hormones, a bloated belly
Rounds of shots, and lots of time watching telly
Until the eggs were retrieved, inserted within
For someone to have a new life to begin

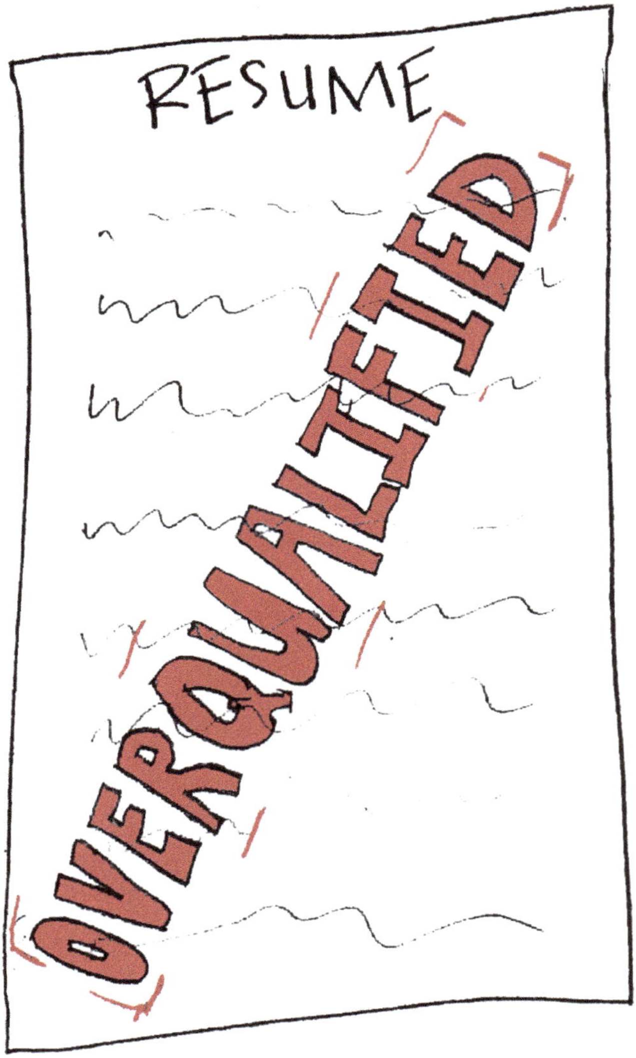
RESUME
OVERQUALIFIED

MAYBE I'M OVERQUALIFIED... THAT'S WHY NO ONE IS HIRING ME?!

I've tweaked and revised
About a trillion times
Chose power adjectives well
So my resume would look swell

It's been sent to companies big and small
Through search engines, emails, and portals
I've received automated responses
I've received no correspondences

Did the email send fail?
Or the wrong button did I press?
At first, I felt confident
But now I feel much less

I refresh my email throughout the day
No missed calls, nothing to say
Maybe the hiring person is away
Or caught in some unexpected dismay

That would surely explain
Why I haven't heard anything
My resume was perfect
My cover letter to a T
Maybe I'm overqualified…
That's why no one is hiring me?

Perhaps the opposite applies
But "underqualified" I choose to deny

THE MODERN WOMAN'S HUNT FOR FOOD

My stomach is growling
I'm starting to shake
It's suddenly dinner time
And I never had a lunch break

So I lunge for my phone
And I start browsing, SEAMLESS
All the snacks I want and more
I still can't believe it!

Where to begin? I don't even know
Asian fusion, pizza, or bento
Crepes, pasta, or sushi
Or maybe a little kimchi

Whatever the case
In a moment's time
This order will be mine, all mine, ALL MINE!

I'll chomp and I'll chew
I'll devour the food through and through
Avert your eyes - it's a sight best unseen
But if I don't eat soon, I'll just be plain mean

There's nothing in the world
That could rip this food away from me
I'd snarl and growl, "I'm hangry, can't you see?"

This is the modern woman's hunt for food

WHEN YOU WEAR DIRTY PANTIES ON YOUR SCARF, IT'S TIME TO REASSESS

My dirty clothes were all around
On the floor and on the ground
Strewn across my bed as I grabbed a scarf in a hurry
To wrap around my neck in a fury

Bounding down the stairs to the subway
I began the journey to my stop far away
I focused my attention on a book
It wasn't until near the end I began to look

Around the carriage to see what I could see
A young girl staring back at me
And a yellow hue below my chin
Almost in slow motion, I peeked down with a grin

Behold, something lacey and yellow
Tucked away in my scarf, saying hello
For a moment, I thought, perplexed "What is this?"
And then like lightening it flashed "Oh my Jesus!"

"It's my dirty panties, twice worn, on my scarf
Strung around my neck, how I want to barf!"
But with a motion so quick and so sly
I used my book to tuck it further inside

Peeking around I wondered who'd seen
But the girl barely blinked, she hadn't seen a thing
I supposed in this city, it's not so uncommon to see
People with dirty laundry out walking the street

ARE YOU A CELEBRITY?

On occasion, I don't wear my glasses
And boy is it a treat!
I always seem to cross paths
With lots of celebrities!

I think they see me too
Because they stare right back

I smile and I wink
I bat my eyes and flirt
And I'm always surprised
By how it makes their head jerk

"ME?" they signal
"Why yes, you," I return
They fidget and grin
Before they run and turn

Of course I can never be certain
If any of this is true
Because without my glasses
I really haven't a clue

But regardless I believe
These happenings are real
It's nice to tell my family
My move here is a big deal

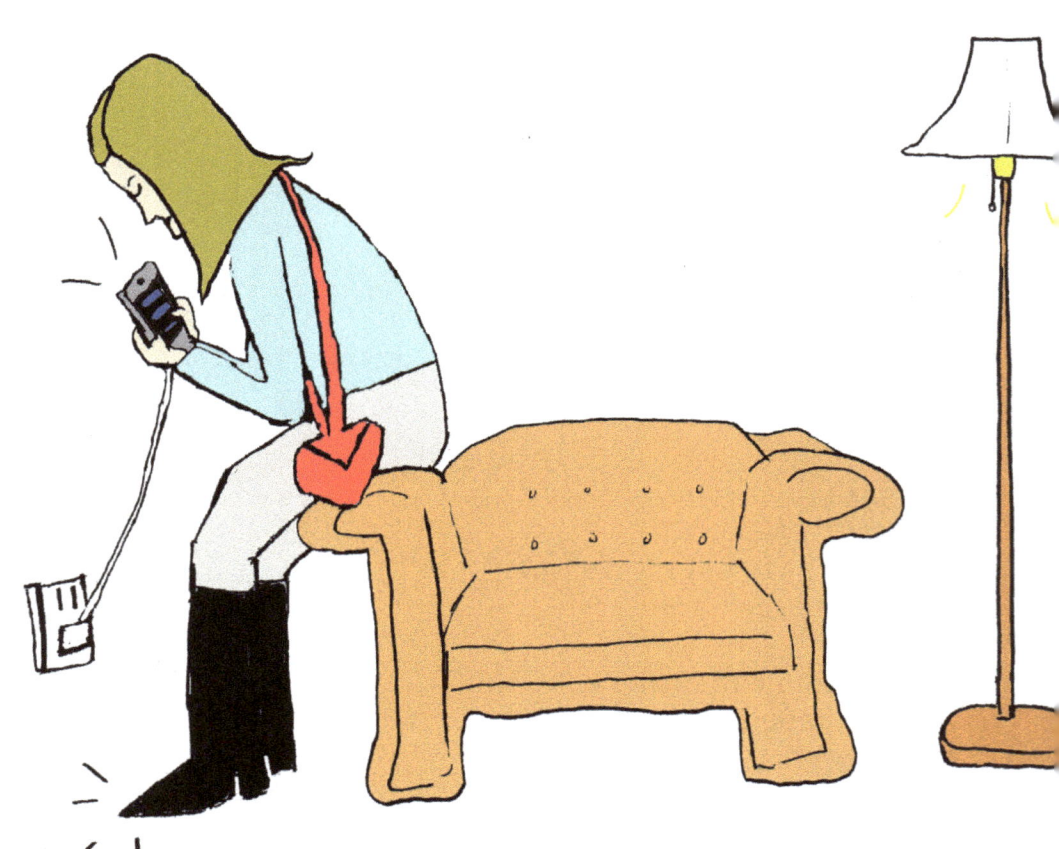

WHAT'S THE PLAN TONIGHT, GUYS?

It's 9pm on Saturday
I'm still waiting on a text
I saw some text bubbles
But no actual details yet

I don't need much, just an o'clock
A clue as to a borough, or a block
A place, a landmark, or a street
Just the basics so we can meet

We discussed it before
As I was walking out the door
You all smiled
And nodded yes

But now it seems
You might have forgot
That we had plans
Or, perhaps, we did not

Anyway, I'm happy to let you all decide
Since I'm new to the group
And making friends can be weird
They're there, then they disappear
So, just curious, what's the plan tonight, guys?

MANAGING A HANGOVER AT WORK

Sometimes it's a given
Like the morning after the office holiday party...
Hangovers for all, they say!
Hangovers for you, Tom, Dick, and Harry!

But other times, it's a secret
For no one else to know
You put on a face
So your pain doesn't show

Try to wash the mascara away
Wear dark shades on the subway
Then swallow an aspirin or two or three
With water, coffee, detox juice please

Stumble into work
With nausea and an aching head
You wonder if it was worth it
You'd much rather be lying in bed

Your just an intern, pretty lady
You'll get through the day
You earn not a penny
Yet just work the day away

Was it worth it, again you ask?
I'd say yes, but don't listen to me
Listen to the grumbles and gripes
From the other employees

CAN I DO A BELATED GAP YEAR?

I should be a mover and shaker
A fire maker and risk taker
Oh how I try and try until my face turns blue
But somehow I only make it a step or two

I lunge my legs forward
Then I get shoved ten feet back
Oh how I try and try until my face turns black

I do nothing right
But I also do nothing wrong
Can someone please tell me
Why this is taking so long?

I should be boasting with success
For everyone to admire
My clock is ticking
Yet there still is no fire

The days rush by, the to-dos all in knots
Can't we just say farewell to this plot?

I'll take a gap year from this career pursuit
I'll explore and explore until I find my own route

In this new place I shall be
The best version of me
I'll be a mover and shaker
A fire maker and risk taker

In my very own way
Each and every day

HELLO STRANGERS, LET ME JOIN YOUR BACHELOR PARTY!

After a comedy show one night
I was eager for an adventure, something to excite
But my friends were all tired, they wanted to sleep
So I just went out solo, to find my own beat

Out to a dance bar I did boldly go
The place was packed, elbow to elbow
I got a whiskey ginger, then scoped out the space
I saw three guys, all gloomy in the face

I struck up a conversation and much to my surprise
They were having a bachelor party, these three sad guys
Of course, I made it my mission to get them to dance
Each of them dancing, each had a chance

Others on the dancefloor joined our moves
I bought rounds of shots to get us in the grooves
Smiling and sweating from all of the fun
We skipped and we sang, everyone

Everything was happy, everything was grand
Then the groom grabbed me by the hand
He'd had several drinks, of this I can be blamed
For what happened next, he should bear no shame

He spun me around, too quick, much too fast
Suddenly I was jerked and sent flying past
All the other dancers, as they gazed in awe
Almost in slow motion, as I did fall

The music stopped swiftly with a screech
As the bachelor boys, shocked, reconvened
I felt suddenly like my damage had been done
So, sneaking out, I said goodbye to no one

But I'll always remember the bachelor boys
Who'd sat looking sad, without a ploy
Until a girl all alone and in need of a smile
Showed them how a bachelor party could be wild

RATS AND PIGEONS ARE YOUR FRIENDS TOO

The night is cold and bold and bright
Yet within my soul I'm having a fight
About things that shouldn't matter or cause a fright
But tonight I think I might

Wander around all quiet, all alone
Making the long journey back home
On this empty boulevard all by myself
I think about if I were something else

A rat or a pigeon, just like I see here
Alone on the street with so much to fear
They wonder what they'll eat, wonder where they'll
sleep
They wonder from whose feet they might have to
retreat

They frantically look for somewhere to dwell
Down or up or sideways they cannot tell
They drag our waste, they eat it too
But when a rat or pigeon, what else can you do?

On my gloomy face emerged a grin, just slight
As I began to understand their little plight
They scurry about, as do I
Wondering, asking, begging why

But a rat or pigeon, certainly has it worse
Because in our eyes, rodents are a curse
Being human and alive simply has its glories
If you look close enough, you'll see all the stories

There are stories of loss, stories of light
Stories of other people alone in the night
Rats and pigeons, and you and me
Just sigh, and grin, and stop all your worries

WHEN ROOMMATES ARE GONE, TRY TO STAY NAKED

It's kind of the best thing
Yes, I really do guarantee
That when your roommates are gone
You should be nakey

Start off with a robe
And then let it all out
Take off those silly clothes
And walk naked all about

Just do what you want
Make a sandwich, or a tea
Enjoy every moment
With your tummy out to see

Watch a movie, cut a rug
Whatever you prefer
You'll have a great time
Of this I'm sure

Just be mindful of the hour
Time can totally zoom
But don't let the roommate find you
Naked in the living room

WHERE ARE MY FUCKING KEYS?

It's very late
And I have to pee
But I cannot find my fucking keys

The roommate is gone
The bars are all closing
I'm pacing the street
But I'd rather be dozing

The night was just blah
Not worth this dilemma
I should have just gone home
With a hot fella

This is my reminder
I'm single as hell
I'm stranded on my stoop
And there's no one to tell

My pockets and purse
I've searched very deep
I'm desperate now for sleep

Where are my fucking keys?

RELATIONSHIPS THAT GO SOUR BECAUSE YOU DON'T WANT JUST SEX

The sex is good, yeah it's really really great
But let's spice things up, and go on a date
A movie, a dinner, a walk down the street
Something to prelude our night in the sheets

You text me last minute, or out of the blue
But what can I say, I do it too
So might I dare propose
We see where this goes?

If we turn things up a tad
Maybe it won't be that bad
But given the look on your face
I'm guessing this is not your pace

No problem, no worries, no foul game
I wish I could say the same
Let's high five and be on our way
I'll go on a date with someone else another day

THE JOY OF MAKING DINNER FOR ONE

Small pot, small serving
No need to make much
But if there's more
Leftovers aren't a fuss

Candles or a movie
Whatever I decide
Because, darlin', it's just me dining here tonight
Smooth jazz or the local news, I entertain as I
choose

And the noises I make
A burp, or a slurp
I don't have to hide
With no one by my side

Make a mess? Don't mind me
There's no one here to see
One and done, or a lengthy meal
I do just as I feel

At first it felt strange and empty
To be eating all alone
But I've come to understand
The joy of making dinner for one

REFUGE FOR LOST SOCKS

It's sort of a mystery
How my sock collection came to be
I never bought a pair, you see
They somehow just find me

One pair striped black and white
Snuck home with me from a guy's one night
After a romantic Valentine's Day
Where we spent the night in the hay

I even have socks that cover each toe
"Toe Socks" they're called, you should give them a go!
They're colorful with spots of red and green
A holiday gift from somebody

Short athletic socks for jogging or such
Are in my drawer, but I haven't the hunch
From where on earth they ran away
Since I never exercise, what can I say?

But perhaps my favorite pair of all
Is this pair that are very tall
Wilderness socks, outstretched and thick
Jumped in my suitcase as I made the switch
From my hometown to NYC
And here I use them for sock puppetry

Some socks are solo, some socks in pairs
Some socks with holes, some socks repaired
But ultimately, I keep them all here
Memories and mysteries to compare

Perhaps I'll never buy socks, I deem
Being a refuge for lost socks is the dream

WHAT KIND OF BODEGA DOESN'T SELL LOOSIES?

It's been one of those days
It's been quite a doozy
What I need right now
Is a loosey

I question life decisions
I feel loads of regret
All I need right now
Is a cigarette

Since I'm not a "smoker"
I rarely buy a pack
I'll just pop into this bodega
I'm sure they've got my back

I gave them a nod and wink
Then slid over 50 cents
But they blinked and blinked
They didn't know what to think

They shrugged, they mumbled
They shook their heads no
"But this is Brooklyn!" I argued, before turning to go

What kind of bodega doesn't sell loosies?!

HOW THE MTA MADE ME CRY

I timed out my whole entire day
Then the subway encountered a delay
Five minutes became ten, ten minutes became thirty
Who knew I'd suddenly be in a hurry

We'd been sitting at the station
For a million years it seemed
The updates were crackly
I muffled a scream

The worst part was right
When hope was in sight
The train switched to local
This must have been some kind of jokal

When you're underground for this much time
You start to form words just to rhyme

Point is, with the added stops, I would be late
Late, late for a very important date
Not a "date" date, just a job interview
In retrospect, I could have taken the N or the Q
Certainly there was some better route

Though life in NYC is hard, I try
This is how the MTA made me cry

SMALL CHRISTMAS TREE JUST FOR ME

My favorite bodega, diagonal to where I am
The best friend even in the early AM

So why not go to this place to retrieve
Each year, my little Christmas tree

Narrow and bare, but eager and full
Of hope for the holidays, and the tidings yule

So little tree, with fairy lights,
Together we'll find all that we delight

Just you, my small Christmas tree
Each year, a wintry joy, just for me

RUN LIKE A FOSTER DOG

Welcome to my apartment, Ella foster dog
You've come a long journey
Let's go out on a jog

You jump, you wiggle, you tap-dance your feet
I throw on some sneakers
To run on the street

It's been such a long time, since I exercised
I might pull a muscle
Or collapse on my side

Yet immediately when we turn on the avenue
You run as fast as you can
I hardly know what to do

With my arm outstretched and the leash pulled
tight
I run as fast as I can
It is quite a sight

My shoes pound and thud with such a loud thunder
The other street walkers stare
They fear a blunder

But miraculously, my feet somehow keep up
I run like you, Ella
I run like a pup

Afterall, for any animal friend in need
In the least I can run
And let you be free

I WAS ASSIGNED AN INTERN THERAPIST AFTER A BREAKDOWN

Working long days, coming home to a roommate
stress
I was doing ok and then something just snapped
One would call it a mental breakdown, I guess

A friend came over, from work he did flee
With calming tea, kind words, and soothing
melodies

The next day I went to get some advice
But being without money, I'd have to suffice

With an intern therapist to be my guide
For a first therapist, I thought, an intern sounds fine!

He really did listen, and seemed to care
Even when I cried and mumbled, he didn't just stare

I wanted to know more about what had enticed
Such an upset and sense of inner poltergeist

I began to understand, or really just to share
Until he graduated on to real patients in despair

But I guess just being a person of fear of myself
Having a friend at the beginning was the perfect
help

So when out of dollars and no therapist to afford
I can at least remember when a friend came to my
door

The first step, however, was giving him a call
If I hadn't reached out, I may not be here at all

THE ART OF DANCING WITH YOURSELF

Late at night
Or in the afternoon
All you need
Is a dance-right tune

Something with a beat
Or just a nice flow
Let your body guide you
It'll show you how to go

Feeling kind of lonely?
Feeling kind of sad?
Just turn up the music, baby
And show yourself the best time you've ever had

No one else is needed
Coincidentally, no one else is around
Just do as Billy suggested
And dance to that sound!

Dance limbs up high
Dance limbs down low
Dance with your plants
And your lamps and fishbowl

Smile from ear to ear
Wiggle your fingers, toes, and rear
Sing if you want
So those outside can hear

Dance until you've forgotten
Why you felt so bad
Show yourself the best time
That you've ever had

SINGLE GIRLS SEEKING BAR FRIENDS

Just the roommate and I at our local watering hole
A weeknight, not too late, just a nice place to say
hello

But there must be something about our faces
The way our eyes, ears, and noses are situated

Because once again a girl has appeared
Alone, broken hearted, lost something dear

She's joined our drinking, our jokes, our laughs
The hours go by, they pass and pass

Until we've made a one-night-stand friend
I guess girls just need friends like us, time and
again

So if you are ever in need, we're here for you
Just go to your local bar, we'll buy you a few

Girls united, always here to lend an ear
Even if afterwards you forever disappear

DID I TELL YOU I HAD A DONUT TODAY?

Today is a special day, haven't you heard?
Why? You ask. Well "donut" is the word!

I never have a craving
No I never really do
But today I woke up with a craving
So I skipped a block or two

Or more like ten
To make it to the right place
The place where they make donuts
Right in front of your face

Since I have that refined hipster taste
Their flavors are quite clever
It was difficult to choose
But I ate a whole damn donut

And now I tell you, you, and you

Sometimes it's the small things
That make you feel like you can sing

But I guess I should be still
Stop skipping all around
Because suddenly the donut
Feels like it won't stay down

Some days I feel special
Some days I feel like a schmuck
But at least today I felt happy
Because of a simple donut

BEWARE OF BENCHES

These shoes I'm wearing sure are cute
They're vintage and leathery – what a hoot!
But man oh man, my feet are not happy
They're not made for feet, which is kind of crappy

My ankles feel wobbly
My toes all scrunched up
My feet are screeching
They are going to erupt

For days, and nights, they will not be satisfied
So I'll take a break on this bench, until they revive
I try to avoid benches most of the time
Mainly because of bed bugs and where they hide

But in this moment I need my feet to rest
So I'll stop here if only for a sec
After I'd sat only a moment or two
Passersby gawked and laughed, for what or for whom?

Glancing down at my feet I thought, "What the fuck?!"
Under my shoes was nothing but gross ugly muck
By "muck" I mean someone else's puke
My first sit on a bench and I encountered this cursed fluke

I jumped up and screamed with such a loud holler
The rats and the pigeons wondered what was the bother
But I shrugged it off, scuffed my shoes about
And then just kept going as if nothing was a shout

Because sometimes things happen,
Oh that is very true
Just don't let other people's puke
Get the best of you

BROOKLYN IS BIG!

FRIENDS OUT OF CONVENIENCE

Bushwick, Bensonhurst,
Red Hook, Williamsburg
Park Slope, Flatbush,
Crown Heights, have you heard?

So many places in Brooklyn
So many people to see
I haven't even mentioned
Places in the city

When I meet someone
A friend, or, even a lover
It's always an important detail
To discover

The subways between their hood and mine
Because, well, there's a line

For how far I'll go to see someone new
What's that, you say, you live nearby?
Well then, my friend, you'll certainly do

HOW ARE WE SUPPOSED TO SWIM WITH ALL THESE STINKING WAVES?

After a journey on the subway
With stinky hipsters, surfers, and castaways
We arrive to the Far Rockaways

In big ridiculous hats, we're here
But the waves are much too debonaire
So the roommate and I just stare in fear

My bathing suit is sexy but a million years old
I don't think there's much more the elastic can hold
I might expose a boob, oh so white and bold

"How are we supposed to swim with all these stinking waves?"
Asked the roommate to me
We both just glare disappointed out to the sea

The water is murky and very very dark
There's most definitely is some suspicious shark
And our bodies it will most definitely tear apart

So instead we try to spread a blanket on the sand
But the stinking wind we just don't understand
It's sending our supplies straight out of our hands

Beach bags on our shoulders, we admit our defeat
We instead go to eat a hotdog and rest our feet
Alas, Coney Island is a challenging place to retreat

But with its wind and waves out of control
Coney Island is still a place to behold
A gathering ground for the young and for the old

We don't have to swim, no we don't even try
We instead enjoy people-watching as they pass by

COME OVER TO MY ROOFTOP, JUST DON'T FALL

In this apartment, where I have dwelled
For many years, no one can tell
That the best part lingers outside
Through the windows where raccoons reside

Come over to my rooftop, out the windows in the
back
Just make sure you stretch, and don't throw out your
back
Lurching through the windowsill to my extended
abode
Escape back on the rooftops of the businesses
below

It's vast and open, with trees peeking over
But there's something that everyone should soon
discover
Is that the line between your fun and its fate
Is not very difficult to navigate

Watch your step, to the right, or the left
There might be a small place to fall, if you haven't
seen it yet
But, here in the urban jungle, outside spaces are
rare
So just mind your feet, don't fall, if you care

As is the warning, here and all about
Because Brooklyn is a labyrinth, you'll soon figure
out

A CLOSE CALL SAILING ON THE HUDSON

With me as first mate, and Avram as Captain
We sailed through the rain back to Manhattan

A storm had caught us out in the fray
So we heaved and we hoed all of the way

Chelsea Piers, our dock, was almost in sight
When we saw something that gave us a fright

A cargo ship suddenly right by our side
The winds pushing us surely to collide

Sailboat sideways, the water just at my toes
Avram moved quickly to grab at the ropes

"Take the wheel!" he shouted out to me
So I did, while he moved fast as I'd ever seen

He dashed in a flash to set the ropes free
And the sailboat fought to follow his lead

In my mind I thought. "This is it, I just might
Have to leap from the boat, into the Hudson I'll dive"

But the wind and sails suddenly obeyed with precision
And we turned, barely missing the cargo ship collision

Out of breath and exhausted, Avram and I
Looked at each other, right in our eyes

Immediately, on our faces, he and I did grin
If we had to do it all over, we'd do it again

Because you never know when a storm may appear
Just think of Captain Avram, and you'll have nothing to fear

BE A NICE HUMAN

It's not so difficult to understand
It's as simple as giving a hand
The basic rules of humankind
Simple acts of niceness to keep in mind

Such as pressing the elevator button for someone
with full arms
A kind gesture, that really causes no harm
Or when a person on the subway could use a seat
Just give yours away, so they can rest their feet

Or when a stranger simply drops some dollars
Pick them up and give the dropper a holler

Be a nice adult, so everyone can see
It'll be the thing they remember to repeat
Soon we'll all be nice people, you and me
It'll be such a treat

You never know
Where all these humans go
Each has struggles, each has pain
So be kind and it might just change their day

It's not so hard, no I really do swear
To be a nice human is nice, if you dare

THE EMERGENCY ROOM AT BELLEVUE ON NYE IS BONKERS

It was just past midnight on New Year's Day
I took an ambulance ride to hell, one might say
The story started with a drink or two
Not very many, I would like to prelude

But the night being oh so dark and frosty
The boyfriend and I decided to do a little joggy
From a party in the Lower East Side
To the East Village where he reside

In high heels and flowy pants
This perhaps was not the best circumstance
I ran and I ran past packed Ubers and cars
But then fell too quickly to catch my scars

Onto the concrete my chin did smack
And when I sat up, my face felt whack
Immediately I knew, my jaw was broken
Looking back, the doctor's disagreement was a token

Three days in the hospital I did stay
Until they could wire my mouth shut, nothing to say
In all of this, I was actually fine
Overcome with the drama of humankind

Bellevue Hospital, if you care to know
Is totally bonkers on NYE, it's a circus show
Handcuffed to beds or wandering in drunken hazes
The admittees were zombies with crazy dazes

So if you did not already care to be kind
Remember there's staff at emergency rooms who mind
Try to avoid smashing your face, our bashing your knee
Because the hospitals have enough drama, let them be
free

But if you do find yourself in some kind of plight
Just be calm, and know, everything will be alright

GROWING UP, STAYING IN, GETTING A CAT

I could go out tonight
Join my friends for a bite
Maybe accept a date from a guy
And even let him buy

Yet there's a certain buddy I'd prefer
To hang out with and rub his fur
I shall name him Gideon, and that is that
He's my amazing new rescue cat

He's oh so sweet and cuddly
I love him, and he loves me doubly
So I'm staying in, and growing up
My best friend eats his food from a cup

DO THEY LOVE ME?

Do they love me?
Of this I can't be sure

But surely I can find something else to adore
A rock, a tree, a breeze, a star
A pet, a lamp, a plant and more
There's so much to love near and far

One thing is true, I can only be me
So choosing what I love is how it shall be
Whether it be flowers, the sky, or a dream

WALNUT STREET
— PUBLISHING —

ABOUT THE AUTHOR

Bonnie Blue Edwards is a filmmaker, producer, and writer based in Brooklyn. Her career took form while working as a producer on The New York Times rave-review play *Helen & Edgar*, a collaboration with the originators of NPR storytelling juggernaut The Moth. She's since been part of the producing team on five stage performances, eight feature films, two live broadcast television events, dozens of commercials, and even an award-winning web-series. Edwards also directed and produced the short documentary *Out In Alabama* which featured Academy Award-winning filmmaker Cynthia Wade as consultant, and served as a conversation piece during the movement for marriage equality. During the 2020 pandemic, she was featured in The New York Times article "All Alone in a Three-Bedroom Apartment" for her unusual living situation in Crown Heights, as well as in VICE for her activism in "What A Typical Week Looks Like for this Mutual Aid Volunteer". She's currently developing an investigative podcast and documentary in her hometown of Birmingham. In her free time, she can be found road-tripping or hiking with her rescue dog named Hope.

Thank you for taking the time to read. Seriously. Please stay in touch through my Instagram account @bonnieblue952 or at my website www.bonnieblueedwards.com.

ABOUT THE BOOK

Stressed Out & Scatterbrained is a collection of poems and illustrations that merge together the gritty entrance to the "real world" and humorous recounts of those human experiences that follow. Captured in both relatable as well as unusual scenarios, the rhyming stories were written in real time over 10 years (saved on crumpled sheets of paper and obscure notebooks) after the writer moved to New York City from Alabama. Topics cover subway mishaps, lost keys, new friends, job hunting, dating, and occurrences of loneliness amidst searching for oneself. Yet, spotted throughout, are stories of discovering resilient ways to stay happy through all of life's punches.

self-doubt, self-deprecation, nervousness, hopefulness, ambition, anxiety, fear, love, and more

www.ingramcontent.com/pod-product-compliance
Lightning Source LLC
Chambersburg PA
CBHW051236120626
46547CB00013B/1674